GENESIS 12-33

THEOLOGY OF WORK   PROJECT

GENESIS
12-33

THE BIBLE AND YOUR WORK
Study Series

HENDRICKSON
PUBLISHERS

Theology of Work
The Bible and Your Work Study Series: Genesis 12–33

ISBN 978-1-61970-623-1

William Messenger, Executive Editor, Theology of Work Project
Sean McDonough, Biblical Editor, Theology of Work Project
Patricia Anders, Editorial Director, Hendrickson Publishers

Contributors:
Christopher Gilbert, "Genesis 12–33" Bible Study
Bob Stallman, "Genesis 12–50 and Work" in the Theology of Work Bible Commentary

The Theology of Work Project is an independent, international organization dedicated to researching, writing, and distributing materials with a biblical perspective on work. The Project's primary mission is to produce resources covering every book of the Bible plus major topics in today's workplaces. Wherever possible, the Project collaborates with other faith-and-work organizations, churches, universities and seminaries to help equip people for meaningful, productive work of every kind.

Printed in the United States of America

First Printing — July 2015

Contents

The Theology of Work

Work is not only a human calling, but also a divine one. "In the beginning God created the heavens and the earth." God worked to create us and created us to work. "The LORD God took the man and put him in the garden of Eden to till it and keep it" (Gen. 2:15). God also created work to be good, even if it's hard to see in a fallen world. To this day, God calls us to work to support ourselves and to serve others (Eph. 4:28).

Work can accomplish many of God's purposes for our lives—the basic necessities of food and shelter, as well as a sense of fulfillment and joy. Our work can create ways to help people thrive; it can discover the depths of God's creation; and it can bring us into wonderful relationships with co-workers and those who benefit from our work (customers, clients, patients, and so forth).

Yet many people face drudgery, boredom, or exploitation at work. We have bad bosses, hostile relationships, and unfriendly work environments. Our work seems useless, unappreciated, faulty, frustrating. We don't get paid enough. We get stuck in dead-end jobs or laid off or fired. We fail. Our skills become obsolete. It's a struggle just to make ends meet. But how can this be if God created work to be good—and what can we do about it? God's answers for these questions must be somewhere in the Bible, but where?

The Theology of Work Project's mission has been to study what the Bible says about work and to develop resources to apply the Christian faith to our work. It turns out that every book of the Bible gives practical, relevant guidance that can help us do our jobs better, improve our relationships at work, support ourselves, serve others more effectively, and find meaning and value in our work. The Bible shows us how to live all of life—including work—in Christ. Only in Jesus can our work be transformed to become the blessing it was always meant to be.

To put it another way, if we are not following Christ during the 100,000 hours of our lives that we spend at work, are we really following Christ? Our lives are more than just one day a week at church. The fact is that God cares about our life *every day of the week*. But how do we become equipped to follow Jesus at work? In the same ways we become equipped for every aspect of life in Christ—listening to sermons, modeling our lives on others' examples, praying for God's guidance, and most of all by studying the Bible and putting it into practice.

This Theology of Work series contains a variety of books to help you apply the Scriptures and Christian faith to your work. This Bible study is one volume in the series The Bible and Your Work. It is intended for those who want to explore what the Bible says about work and how to apply it to their work in positive, practical ways. Although it can be used for individual study, Bible study is especially effective with a group of people committed to practicing what they read in Scripture. In this way, we gain from one another's perspectives and are encouraged to actually *do* what we read in Scripture. Because of the direct focus on work, The Bible and Your Work studies are especially suited for Bible studies *at* work or *with* other people in similar occupations. The following lessons are designed for thirty-minute lunch breaks, although they can be used in other formats as well.

Christians today recognize God's calling to us in and through our work—for ourselves and for those whom we serve. May God use this book to help you follow Christ in every sphere of life and work.

Will Messenger, Executive Editor
Theology of Work Project

Introduction:
Abraham to Jacob

In chapters 12 through 33 of Genesis, we discover how God turns a nomad family into a people for himself through whom he will bless all of humanity. Beginning with just two people—Abram and Sarai—God invests himself intimately in this family, teaching them his ways, growing their numbers, building their capabilities, leading them through peril, triumph, and suffering, and preparing them to change the world. The ultimate blessing this family brings is the birth of Jesus Christ, the Son of God, but that lies far in the future from the point of view of Genesis. In these chapters of the story, the focus is on learning how to live and work as God's people. The guidance God gives them in their work is still powerful guidance for us in our work today.

In this Bible study, we pick up in the book of Genesis where the Bible study of Genesis chapters 1 to 11 left off. Whereas the first eleven chapters told the universal story of all humankind, chapter 12 opens with the Lord's call to a particular man, Abram, and his wife Sarai (who are later renamed Abraham and Sarah). The work life of Abraham and Sarah, their son Isaac and his family, and Isaac's sons Esau and Jacob form this second part of Genesis, ending with chapter 33. Chapters 34 through 50 of Genesis carry on the story with Jacob's children, especially Joseph, and their descendants, which will be discussed in a separate Bible study.

So here, we come alongside the first three generations of the family, generations of people who struggle to make a living, endure social upheaval, raise children in safety, and remain faithful to God. Their story is surely similar to our own experiences. On occasion, they reflect virtue learned in relation to their God, yet they repeatedly fall into behaviors that hurt themselves and others. Through it all, God remains faithful to his covenant to bless them in all circumstances, despite the gravity of their many failures.

By God's grace they do bless others in the lands where they wander. Even more so today as we follow in their footsteps, our work can be a blessing to those around us.

Chapter 1

Abraham—Journey from Haran to Egypt

(Genesis 12:1–13:2)

Lesson #1: Unlike Babel (12:1–3)

The story begins with God calling Abraham into a covenant of faithful service.

> Now the LORD said to Abram, "Go from your country and your kindred and your father's house to the land that I will show you. And I will make of you a great nation, and I will bless you and make your name great, so that you will be a blessing. I will bless those who bless you, and him who dishonors you I will curse, and in you all the families of the earth shall be blessed." (12:1–3)

By obedience to God's call, Abraham distinguishes himself sharply from those who participate in the Babel enterprise. There are at least five contrasts to consider.

First, Abraham trusts God for guidance, significance, and security, rather than human skill and ingenuity.

Second, the builders seek fame on their own terms (11:4), but Abraham trusts God's promise that he will make Abraham's name great (12:2), not for his own sake, but in order that "all the families of the earth shall be blessed" (12:3).

Third, Abraham is willing to go wherever God leads him, the original entrepreneur, always moving on to fresh endeavors, in new locations. The builders of Babel create their project to centralize the population around them (11:4). In doing so, they reject God's purpose for humanity to "fill the earth" (1:28). The outcome of Abraham's faithfulness blesses us even today. But Babel is a byword for futility.

 Food for Thought

From the first three contrasts between Abraham and the Babel enterprise, what do you think is similar in faithful work and work done without faith? What makes it different? Can you illustrate it from your own work life?

_____

_____

_____

_____

_____

_____

_____

_____

Fourth, Abraham demonstrates that God's design is for people to work in healthy networks of relationships. He and his family build good relationships (21:22–34; 23:1–12), as they are willing to trust God among strangers in the land of Canaan (17:8). But the tower builders seek to guard themselves in a fortress.

Fifth, Abraham takes a long-term view. God's promises were to be realized only in the time of Abraham's offspring. The Apostle Paul interprets the "offspring" to be Jesus (Gal. 3:19), more than a thousand years after Abraham. And still, the completion of this promise awaits Jesus' return (Matt. 24:30–31). Progress toward this goal can't be measured by quarterly reports! But the tower builders took no thought for how their project would affect future generations, and God criticized them explicitly for this lapse (11:6).

 Food for Thought

What does a healthy network of relationships look like in your work experience? What short-term benefits come from your work, for you and those you serve? What about long-term benefits? What legacy do you hope it provides?

_____

_____

_____

_____

_____

_____

_____

_____

To summarize: Abraham realizes that any attempt to grasp at God's promised blessing in his own power is futile. His practice is to trust God's guidance and provision (22:8–14). Although these promises are not fully realized by the end of the book of

Genesis, they initiate the covenant between God and the people of God through which the redemption of the world will come to completion in the day of Christ (Phil. 1:10).

And so Abraham's faithfulness flows through the work of his livelihood as blessing. It begins on the local level, with occupational skills such as shepherding, tent-making, military protection, and preparing and trading in animal products. Following this, the nations descending from Abraham develop the arts of parenting and relationships, politics, literacy, diplomacy, administration, education, economics, the healing arts, and other occupations. To ensure the blessings of work flow to all peoples, God calls Abraham and his descendants to "walk before me, and be 'blameless'" (17:1). This requires developing the arts and skills of worship and religious instruction for the people of God and service to the world at large.

Prayer

Pause for a few moments of silence to reflect on this lesson. Then offer a prayer, either spontaneous or by using the following:

> *Lord,*
>
> *You are the One more faithful than Abraham. Teach us to cast ourselves upon you as Abraham did, willing to journey through the wider world, trusting in your provision for each step of the journey. Help us to appreciate the breathtaking scope of your purposes in the diversity of work you have given us to do. We offer it back to you and trust you to make it significant for eternity.*
>
> *Amen.*

Lesson #2: Pastoral Life (12:4–7)

A recurring image in the stories of Abraham, Isaac, and Jacob is the great wealth they accumulate by careful animal husbandry. Yet there are also droughts that force them to use their wealth simply to survive. The alluring magnet to which Abraham, Isaac, and Jacob are drawn for family survival is the nearest center of commerce, the Egyptian empire.

In their work as herders of sheep, goats, cattle, donkeys, and camels, they rely on something that can assist small businesses even today—large families. We know Abraham leaves Haran with his wife Sarah, his nephew Lot, and an unspecified number of people and possessions (12:5). They soon become prosperous, measured by their servants or "staff," the size of their herds, and the silver and gold that come from trading in animals and their products of wool, milk, leather, and meat (12:16; 13:2; 27:9; 31:38).

The family becomes so successful that eventually Abraham and Lot need to separate their herds and send their families in different directions so as not to overtax the available land (13:11).

 Food for Thought

Have you ever experienced a family business or a business run like a family? What are its upsides and downsides? How does this relate to the fortunes of Abraham's family?

_____

_____

_____

_____

_____

Seminomads assess the availability of usable pasture and water, with intimate knowledge of seasonal weather and geography. They settle in an area long enough to grow crops and trade with those living in more settled communities. Their herds require skillful handling and even military protection. And the profits are measured not primarily by individual wealth, but by the well-being work brings to the entire family and their servants. Similarly, the effects of famine come at a cost to all.

In this environment, individuals certainly have their own responsibilities and are accountable for their actions, but the communal nature of the family business contrasts with today's culture of personal achievement and the expectation of ever-increasing profits. Social responsibility is the primary concern of the family of Abraham.

 Food for Thought

As you consider what was required for Abraham's family to succeed at their work, what kinds of wisdom and experience are necessary to be successful in your own work? How is this wisdom attained?

_____

_____

_____

_____

_____

In this seminomadic way of life, shared values are essential. Mutual dependence and awareness of common ancestry build solidarity, but they can also prompt vengeful justice imposed upon anyone who might disrupt its code of honor (34:25–31). Tribal leaders tap the wisdom of the group in order to make sound decisions. They develop communication systems for their shepherds, who can lead the animals more than a day's walk from the main camp (37:12–13). They promote conflict resolution in order to settle disputes peaceably with local people (26:19–22). As honorable people, they provide hospitality to strangers to keep them safe from outlaw groups.

By these means, the family business of Abraham and Sarah prospers, even with years of reversal through extended famines (12:10–11; 13:2; 26:13; 31:1; 41:53–57). As evidence of their wealth, consider Jacob's extravagant gift from his herds to his estranged brother, Esau (32:13–15).

Jacob credits God for this bounty; while conferring blessings on his sons near his death, he says that the God of his fathers has been "my shepherd all my life long to this day" (48:15). In other biblical books, we are warned that a love of material wealth is a stumbling block to faithfulness (e.g., Jer. 17:11; Hab. 2:5; Matt. 6:24), but here we learn that God does not begrudge his people prosperity as a consequence of their faithful, diligent work.

 Food for Thought

How does the list of shared values above relate to values statements, expressed or implied, in your workplace?

_____

_____

_____

_____

_____

Prayer

Pause for a few moments of silence to reflect on this lesson. Then offer a prayer, either spontaneous or by using the following:

> *Lord,*
>
> *Grant that we will value our opportunities to participate with you in our work, and help us to bring prosperity to our region for the sake of many communities with which we have to deal. Keep us trusting you, even in seasons of difficulty, so that we don't surrender to the distorted or short-term values we may find in our workplaces.*
>
> *Amen.*

Lesson #3: Disaster in Egypt (12:8–13:2)

Careful reading of the terse account of Abraham's travels in this passage reveals that it is difficult for Abraham upon arrival in Canaan. He faces competition for land (12:6), and he looks for a place he can freely occupy (12:8–9). Eventually, a famine forces his hand and he pulls out entirely, taking his family to the economic hub of Egypt, hundreds of miles from the land of God's promise (12:10).

He is vulnerable as an economic refugee, and he suffers that fear of exploitation common to immigrants who bear the stigma of being regarded as "alien" by the citizens of the land. His wife Sarah is so beautiful that he expects the Egyptians might murder him to obtain her. So he tells Sarah to claim that she is his sister rather than his wife.

Abraham's fears come true when no less than Pharaoh desires Sarah, and so she is "taken into Pharaoh's house" (12:15). As a result, "the LORD afflicted Pharaoh and his house with great plagues" (12:17). When Pharaoh discovers that he has taken another man's wife, he acts honorably and returns Sarah to Abraham with orders to depart his country (12:18–19). He had paid Abraham an astonishing "bride price," with large gifts of sheep and cattle, male and female donkeys, male and female servants, camels (12:16), and silver and gold (13:2). The family that arrived in desperate straits departs with their original wealth restored.

 Food for Thought

What do you think God is saying to Abraham by gifting him so richly with royal booty, when it is clear that Abraham has acted fearfully and faithlessly? How does this relate to God's original promise to Abraham?

_____

_____

_____

_____

_____

_____

_____

_____

This encounter in Egypt graphically warns us of the moral dilemmas we may face when wealth is reversed and poverty threatens. It is normal that such stress tests our faith in God our provider.

Although Abraham and Sarah are fleeing starvation, how could Abraham subject his wife to an illicit sexual liaison with Pharaoh? In an information age we know that millions of women and girls today are traded sexually to support their impoverished families. God punishes Pharaoh because of this vulnerable woman and her family.

Pharaoh in his state of shame berates Abraham for misrepresenting Sarah's identity. But God does not accept Pharaoh's excuse. When Abraham does the same thing again later with king Abimelech (Gen. 20:7–17), God honors Abimelech for declining to receive Sarah into his bed.

In both episodes, God places the responsibility for sexual exploitation squarely with the intended recipient. Pharaoh—who willingly believes that Sarah is happy to engage in the liaison—is punished, while Abimelech—who takes the trouble to uncover the ruse—is praised. God even moves Abimelech to rescue Sarah and her family from their situation, so they are no longer in danger of sexual exploitation.

Abraham's vulnerability and fear make his actions understandable. Nonetheless, Abraham had received God's direct promise: "I will make of you a great nation" (12:2). Why did Abraham's faith in God to make good on his promises fail so quickly? Did survival really require him to lie and direct his wife to become a concubine, or would God have provided another way? Abraham's fears seem to eclipse his trust in God's faithfulness.

Many of us know that path—convincing ourselves that our only choice is between two evils. We surrender ourselves to action that in other circumstances we know is wrong. It would take many more years for Abraham to realize that an unpleasant, but faithful, choice is nonetheless the best option in light of God's promises—rather than to plead powerlessness and surrender to evil, as if there were no choice. Even so, God does not say anything against Abraham or Sarah for falling into sexual exploitation. Instead, he listens to their prayers (Gen. 20:17). God's compassion for them leads to rescue, not judgment.

 Food for Thought

Have you found yourself tested financially through a job or career reversal? If so, what fears or anxieties did you navigate and how did you find your way? What pitfalls did you discover along the way? If not, imagine for a moment what losing your job or closing your business—or wondering how you will even survive—might be like. Consider the unpleasant choices you might be faced with. How does faith in Christ, Abraham's offspring, inform the strategy you might employ to deal with a reversal in your work, career, or job?

_____

_____

_____

_____

_____

_____

_____

_____

Prayer

Pause for a few moments of silence to reflect on this lesson. Then offer a prayer, either spontaneous or by using the following:

> *Lord,*
>
> *You taught us to pray, "Give us this day our daily bread" and "deliver us from evil" (Matt. 6:11, 13). We look to you for sustenance in good times and in bad, and we ask that you keep us faithful when we find ourselves in difficulties that seem insurmountable. We pray for your compassion and rescue in our times of failure. With you, all things are possible.*
>
> *Amen.*

Chapter 2

Abraham—Faithful in Canaan

(Genesis 13:3–18; 18:1–15)

Lesson #1: Parting with Lot (13:3–18)

Abraham and his family reenter Canaan perhaps wealthier than before the famine. Because the original inhabitants remain in the land, however, the difficulties from which he had fled under duress of drought remain to be overcome. Pastures and water for his family's large herds must be found outside the already occupied areas.

It is worth noting that Abraham returns to the place where he had memorialized God's original covenant with him—as if to start again and this time get it right.

The first issue that arises is within the family business. In the region around Bethel, the herdsmen for Abraham and those of his nephew Lot compete for the grazing territory, with growing friction. Abraham needs to figure out a way to resolve the conflict.

Abraham makes a remarkable offer to his nephew, giving him first choice of the grazing land in the region. The central ridge of land in Canaan is rocky and semiarid, and doesn't support intensive grazing. Lot's eye falls instead to the east and the plain around the Jordan River, which he regards to be "like the garden of the Lord," so he chooses this more prosperous route for his family and livestock (13:10).

 *Food for Thought*

Have you ever avoided a situation rather than face it, only to have it emerge again further along in your life? What do you think made Abraham return to his beginning place? What had changed for him? How would you apply that to a work situation you have faced or would like to face again differently?

_____

_____

_____

_____

_____

_____

_____

Abraham seems to have gained some wisdom from his Egyptian sojourn. He has received a second chance at obedience through God's compassion and material generosity, in the rescue of his wife from Pharaoh's harem. Humbled and with renewed faith, he is not looking out for his own interests but gives preference to his nephew. No matter the future fortunes of either camp, Abraham's decision to give Lot first choice in the matter of territory provides the opportunity for good will and trust between the families as they go their separate ways.

In Luke 19:19, when Zacchaeus the tax collector welcomed Jesus into his home and promised to give half of his possessions to the poor and to repay four times over to the people he had cheated, Jesus called him a "son of Abraham" for his generosity and fruit of repentance (Luke 19:9).

Zacchaeus was responding, of course, to the relational generosity of Jesus, who had confounded the locals by opening his heart to a detested tax collector. Generosity is often derided, or pegged as a weakness or a handicap in life, but especially so in business. Yet, when we receive it, such a gift provides us reason to reconsider our judgment of ourselves in relation to the giver. Unconditional generosity upends mistrust and even old enmities, and it is as valuable in business as it is in family relationships. Perhaps nothing establishes trust and good relationships as solidly as generosity. Colleagues, customers, suppliers, even adversaries, will respond strongly to generosity and remember it for a long time. Closely allied to generosity is hospitality—another development in Abraham's character visible in our next story.

 Food for Thought

The kind of generosity we see in Abraham is often hidden from sight in the marketplace. Generous people in business are like shy rare birds—it takes careful observation to discern their presence. Much that pretends to be generous is merely sharp marketing inducement to buy—such as reward points for credit cards, supermarkets, and airlines. Can you identify a genuine case of generosity in your work experience? If so, how did it change your attitude toward the person or the business?

_____

_____

_____

_____

_____

_____

Prayer

Pause for a few moments of silence to reflect on this lesson. Then offer a prayer, either spontaneous or by using the following:

> *Lord,*
>
> *We remember the words of the Apostle Paul: "[We] comfort those who are in any affliction, with the comfort with which we ourselves are comforted by God" (2 Cor. 1:4). Help us to have a generosity of spirit that overflows from your generous forgiveness and renewal. Help us reject the world's lie of entitlement enough to acknowledge that every good gift comes from you and that we have been generously treated. Grant us hearts made thankful for daily new beginnings.*
>
> *Amen.*

Lesson #2: Hospitality toward Strangers (18:1–15)

The seminomadic life of the ancient world brought people from different clans into contact with one another. Canaan was a natural land bridge between Asia and Africa, and therefore a popular trade route that passed by fortified cities and towns.

The wilderness between settlements was dangerous not only because of predatory animals, but also because of opportunistic bands of outlaws. So it was important for those living in cities and encampments to welcome strangers passing through, protecting them from any danger. These obligations were designed to maintain the honor of persons, their households, and communities. They were a buffer against anarchy.

The following outline of the hospitality code of that period assists us in understanding the way Abraham and Sarah received the visit of the three "men" in Genesis 18. It sets these rules regarding the defined zone around a settlement or encampment.

1. In this zone, the residents must offer hospitality to strangers.

2. The stranger must align as an ally by accepting the offer of hospitality.

3. Only the male head of household or a male citizen may offer such hospitality.

4. The invitation may include a time limit, but this can then be extended if agreeable to both parties on the renewed invitation of the host.

5. The stranger has the right of refusal, but hostilities could ensue if the stranger meant it as an affront to the host's honor.

6. Once the invitation is accepted, the roles of the host and the guest are set by more ancient custom. The guest must not request anything. The host provides the best he has available, despite a modest initial offer. The guest is expected to reciprocate immediately with news, predictions of good fortune, or expressions of gratitude for what he has been given, and praise of the host's generosity and honor. The host must not ask personal questions of the guest, and any such disclosure is at the guest's discretion (as illustrated in Genesis 18:1–15).

7. The guest remains under the protection of the host until he/she leaves the zone of obligation of the host.

 *Food for Thought*

Consider the way in which hospitality is practiced in your workplace or business. Describe the code of honor that seems to underlie it. What elements of the ancient code do you see that continue in our contemporary attitude to hospitality? How would you rewrite this code for your workplace?

_____

_____

_____

_____

_____

_____

_____

When Abraham encounters "the LORD," along with two angels, all appearing as men, he invites them to stay for a feast of the best food he can prepare for them. His behavior is the origin of the New Testament exhortation: "Do not neglect to show hospitality to strangers, for thereby some have entertained angels unawares" (Heb. 13:2).

One small way we might find ourselves continuing in the ancient tradition of hospitality is that when visitors are "on our turf" and we take them out for dinner, we pay for their meals. Why? Because at some deep level we sense that "it's the right thing to do."

Like generosity, hospitality can upend distrust between people and provide opportunity to experience one another in new ways—beyond the expectations and limitations of past experiences.

Hospitality fosters good relationships. When people break bread together, or enjoy recreation or entertainment, they often grow to understand and appreciate each other better. Better working relationships and more effective communication are often fruits of hospitality.

In Abraham and Sarah's time, hospitality was almost always offered in the host's home. Today this is not always possible, or even desirable, and the hospitality industry has come into being to facilitate and offer hospitality in a wide variety of ways. If you want to offer hospitality and your home is too small or your cooking skills too limited, you can take someone to a restaurant or hotel and enjoy camaraderie and deepening relationships there, aided by cooks, servers, and others who have the opportunity to offer hospitality in their own right, as well. Offering hospitality to others can be an act of love, friendship, compassion and social engagement. The example of Abraham and Sarah shows that this work can be profoundly important as a service to God and humanity.

A more contemporary illustration of the power of hospitality is found in the 1987 Danish film *Babette's Feast*, based on an Isak Dinesen story of how a refugee from the French Revolution is received into the community of a small Scandinavian fishing village. The people who accept her in, and whom she seeks to serve, live sectarian lives inside their own small circle. But beneath their public piety fester damaged relationships and bitterness and hurts from unresolved conflicts. By way of thanking them for their hospitality, Babette uses her entire amount of a large lottery win combined with her mastery of French cuisine to provide the church folk and other guests with an extravagant feast. As the villagers enjoy such grand hospitality for the first time, the old walls come down and they experience joy around the table. As a result, healing and reconciliation begin. Depicted in this story is the biblical hospitality which culminates in the wedding feast of Scripture's ultimate promise. The Apostle Peter experiences it over a humble breakfast with Jesus on a beach—reconciliation through Jesus' cooking of a meal by which he communicates to Peter his deep love and forgiveness (John 21:9–19).

Abraham and Sarah experience hospitality in reverse, as they fulfill the obligation to entertain their visitors. The Lord is now present, face to face and approachable. His announcement that elderly Sarah will soon become pregnant is an extravagant gift. The encounter provokes new boldness in Abraham as host. He intercedes on behalf of his nephew Lot, who now resides in the city of Sodom—a city the visitors suggest they will soon destroy. The Lord honors Abraham's respectful but pressing personal questions with direct answers. Between them is now a deeper and more profound relationship. And this too has implications for life at work.

 Food for Thought

In networking for sales, managing staff, getting to know your boss, or developing business or professional relations, how often do you go out for a meal or coffee with those you would like to know better? Can you tell a story of a relationship that changed because of providing or receiving hospitality in this context? How does the "hospitality industry" play into providing or receiving hospitality? What are some real advantages of professional hospitality, and what might be considered its downside?

_____

_____

_____

_____

_____

_____

_____

_____

Prayer

Pause for a few moments of silence to reflect on this lesson. Then offer a prayer, either spontaneous or by using the following:

Lord,

It is amazing that you want to greet us face to face as you did with Abraham and Peter, to name just two. And that you, as the psalmist writes, "prepare a table before me in the presence of my enemies" (Ps. 23:4). Please help us to value hospitality as you do and to offer it as our habit to those who need it, even in our workplaces.

Amen.

Chapter 3

Abraham—Doing Business in Canaan

(Genesis 20:1–18; 21:22–34; 23:1–20)

Lesson #1: Dispute with Abimelech (20:1–18; 21:22–34)

It becomes clear in this Genesis story that when a stranger enters the domain of a king, whatever might be most valuable to the temporary sojourner is carefully inspected for its value to the reigning monarch. A price, if you like, for obligatory protection in the zone of the king's territory. It's an underlying coercion of the vulnerable visitor. In fear for his life again, Abraham says that the beautiful Sarah is his sister, and once again she is taken as the concubine of the king. But the Philistine king, Abimelech, has inadvertently violated the honor rules of hospitality by taking a man's wife.

Mercifully, he is warned in a dream of his impending violation. Once again, God is active for his own purposes and forces the issue with this king by shutting the wombs of the women of his harem. As restitution, Abimelech immediately returns Sarah to her husband and awards Abraham free grazing and water rights to whatever land he wants (20:1–16).

Subsequently, a dispute erupts over a certain well that Abraham had originally dug but Abimelech's herdsmen have now seized (21:25). When Abimelech hears Abraham's complaint, he pleads ignorance of the situation. Although this may or may not be true, the question is how to keep the king accountable to his word. Abraham then initiates a sworn agreement, a treaty that publicly acknowledges Abraham's right to the well and therefore his continued business activity in the region (21:27–31).

 Food for Thought

Those in power often try to coerce others into unfair terms of business. Governments may impose onerous conditions as the price of a license or permit. Corrupt officials may demand bribes. Companies may garner monopolies and drive up prices. Describe experiences you have had of unjust conditions you've faced in the course of gaining a license, project, or job. How did you handle it, and how might you handle it in the future?

_____

_____

_____

_____

_____

_____

_____

It takes hard-earned wisdom to know when to resort to legal redress, and when to act with apparent generosity of spirit. We see in Abraham this capacity for appropriate action. He can be shrewd in apparent generosity (14:22–24). Yet here, Abraham doggedly protects what is his. After all, his family's well-being depends on freedom to graze his herds in an already settled land. This has been the thorny issue of his seminomadic life from the day he arrived in Canaan (12:6; 13:7).

The narrator does not imply that Abraham's resort to law is another wavering in faith, for the account concludes with worship (21:33). Rather, we see a wise and industrious person who conducts his business openly, for the good of all, and makes fair use of appropriate legal protections. Access to water is the primary issue for his flocks, and he is duty bound to protect his business from the dishonorable behavior of the king's herders.

 Food for Thought

In your work, where do you draw the line between "turning the other cheek" and seeking legal protection from exploitation? Why? Is it possible both to protect yourself and to be hospitable and generous to others? How?

_____

_____

_____

_____

_____

_____

A decision to invoke legal or administrative protections is not only a matter of who is in the right, but also of how the decision will affect relationships. When dividing the land with Lot, Abraham's willing surrender of first choice to Lot flows from the sensibility of a renewed faith—that the God who redeemed him from his near disaster in Egypt with abundant wealth will continue to provide for his family's needs. In these circumstances, giving Lot first pick of the pathways is an expression of generosity from his trust in God, and perhaps a growing distrust of his own sense of direction. It improves his relationship with Lot, no doubt, and it certainly deepens his relationship with God.

But by demanding access to the well according to his treaty rights, Abraham ensures the resources needed to keep his family enterprise functioning in Canaan where God has sent him. There will be no more searching for better fortune in other lands! In addition, it seems that Abraham's assertiveness actually improves his relationship with Abimelech. Remember that the original dispute between them arose because Abraham didn't assert his status as a husband when first encountering the king (20:2).

 Food for Thought

Abraham now seems to make his relationship with God primary, including the commission he received, and this influences his demand for legal redress. What experience have you had in asserting yourself in the face of an injustice in your workplace or business? What was the outcome? Would you do anything differently next time?

_____

_____

_____

_____

_____

_____

Prayer

Pause for a few moments of silence to reflect on this lesson. Then offer a prayer, either spontaneous or by using the following:

Lord,

So often we are afraid of conflict and run from it. Teach us the wisdom to know when to stand and protect the work to which you have called us, and when to walk away from perceived threats that are no threat at all. Help us not to lean on our own understanding only, but to turn to you for guidance in everything.

Amen.

Lesson #2: A Family Tomb for Sarah (23:1–20)

We're near the end of Abraham's part in the story of the Promised Land. When Sarah dies, Abraham engages in an exemplary negotiation to buy a burial plot for her. He conducts the negotiations openly and honestly in the presence of witnesses, taking due care for the needs of both himself and the seller (23:10-13, 16, 18).

The property in question is clearly identified (23:9) and Abraham's intended use as a burial site is mentioned several times (23:4, 6, 9, 11, 13, 15, 20).

The dialogue of the negotiation is exceptionally clear, socially proper, and transparent, taking place at the city gate where business was publically conducted. Abraham initiates the request for a real-estate transaction. The local Hittites offer a choice tomb, pro bono—no charge. Abraham demurs, asking them to contact a certain owner of a field with a cave appropriate for a burial site so that he can buy it for the "full price."

Ephron, the owner, overhears the request and offers the field as a gift. There is no security of future ownership in this for Abraham. So he politely offers to pay market value for it.

 Food for Thought

At the death of Sarah—after all the years of life in Canaan—the family business is without a permanent landholding. It hardly looks secure. What is the significance of Abraham's transaction with Ephron, and is it relatable to your own experience in work, career, or business as one called by God?

_____

_____

_____

_____

_____

_____

_____

_____

Contrary to the staged bargaining that was typical of business transactions (Prov. 20:14), Abraham immediately agrees to Ephron's price and pays it "according to the weights current among the merchants" (23:16). In other words, the deal conforms to the standard for silver used in real estate sales.

Perhaps Abraham is so wealthy that he doesn't need to bargain, but it is equally likely he wants a measure of goodwill along with the land. More simply, it may be that he wants to secure an unarguable right to the land, in the face of the besetting issue that "the Canaanites were in the land" (12:6; 13:7). They have the rights that accrue from prior residency and ownership.

Ultimately, he receives the deed to the property with its cave and trees (23:20). It later becomes the burial site not only of Sarah, but also Abraham himself, as well as that of Isaac and Rebekah, Jacob and Leah, and the repatriated bones of Joseph. It is also a "by faith" assertion of the awaited fulfillment of God's promise to give ownership of the whole land to Abraham through his descendants.

So even in this real estate transaction, Abraham's actions flow from his trust in God and in God's vocational commission to him. From that relationship we see the resulting values of integrity, transparency, and business acumen that lead to his enhanced reputation in the land. He is seen as respectful of his family and local business custom and generous in his terms. He is recognized as an honorable yet shrewd negotiator equal in status with the Hittite landholders. He gives his descendants a legacy of landholding to which they can return as its rightful owners in whatever future God has planned.

 Food for Thought

The Spirit of God encompasses time from its beginning to its end. For us, however, bound by time, it can be important to create milestones in our work life and careers as we aim for goals that might yet be far off. What are you aiming for that will take time to blossom? How can you negotiate honestly to obtain what you, your colleagues, or your co-workers need in order to progress toward its fulfillment?

_____

_____

_____

_____

_____

_____

_____

_____

Prayer

Pause for a few moments of silence to reflect on this lesson. Then offer a prayer, either spontaneous or by using the following:

Lord,

Help us in our own call to work to value small beginnings. Draw us forward as faithful men and women who will represent your purposes in all the transactions we undertake.

Amen.

Chapter 4

Isaac—Maintaining the Family Business

(Genesis 21:1–7; 22:1–19; 24:62–67; 25:7–26:35; 27:1–46)

Lesson #1: Defending the Wells
(21:1–7; 22:1–19; 24:62–67; 25:7–18)

Isaac is the son of a great father and the father of a great son, but his own record is mixed. In contrast to the sustained prominence that Genesis gives to Abraham, the life of Isaac is an interlude between the stories of Abraham and Jacob. And the characterization of Isaac's life swings between his faithfulness and his folly. His faithfulness positively maintains the family's business. But God, in order to preserve his covenant with Abraham and Abraham's descendants, must overrule Isaac's petty preference for his eldest son. In Isaac's story, the blessing of the nations through the family line hangs in the balance.

Isaac's life begins as a miracle. Sarah is well beyond the age of fertility, but the promise made by the Lord face-to-face with Abraham comes to pass within a year. Abraham and Sarah treasure Isaac and pass on their faith and values.

As a child, Isaac learns an early lesson in trust and obedience to God and his promises when by all appearances he is about to be slain as a human sacrifice. Abraham binds him, saying, "God will provide for himself the lamb for a burnt offering, my son" (22:8). Abraham's faith is rewarded, and the boy Isaac is freed! Later, God reiterates to Isaac the promises that he once delivered to his father. In so doing, God honors Isaac's succession as patriarch of the family enterprise.

 Food for Thought

Christian life begins with the rescue of each of us as dramatic as Isaac's. Think about how life has been different for you since you first became a believer. How does your faith equip you to walk now in the world of your work?

Throughout most of his life, Isaac follows in Abraham's footsteps. Expressing the same faith, Isaac prays for his childless wife (25:21). Just as Abraham gave an honorable burial to Sarah, together Isaac and Ishmael bury their father (25:9). Isaac becomes such a successful farmer and shepherd that the local population envies him and asks him to move away (26:12–16). He reopens the wells that had been dug during the time of his father, which again became the subject of dispute with the people of Gerar concerning water rights (26:17–21). And, like Abraham, Isaac enters into a sworn agreement with Abimelech about treating one another fairly (26:26–31).

The writer of Hebrews noted that by faith Isaac lived in tents and blessed both Jacob and Esau (Heb. 11:8–10, 20). In short, Isaac inherited a large family business and considerable wealth. Like his father, he did not hoard it but fulfilled the role that God had chosen for him to pass on the blessing that would extend to all nations.

In these positive events, Isaac was a responsible son who learned how to lead the family and to manage its business in a way that honored the faithfulness and better practices of his father. It was no accident. By passing on the story of his walk with God to Isaac, and modeling the values he had learned, Abraham's preparation for succession brought blessing to his enterprise once again.

 Food for Thought

How deliberate is succession planning in your workplace? What skills and values would you want to be modeled for those coming after you? What are, or might be, the benefits to your workplace from grooming the next generation for your tasks?

Prayer

Pause for a few moments of silence to reflect on this lesson. Then offer a prayer, either spontaneous or by using the following:

Lord,

Since you rescued us by providing the one perfect Lamb of God to take away our sin, we have followed after you with our varied gifts and abilities seeking to serve you faithfully. Please, bring to us models of faithfulness in work, and make us into models of faithfulness so that we too ensure the ongoing blessing of the nations.

Amen.

Lesson #2: Ensuring Succession (25:19–26:35)

When Isaac is one hundred years old, it becomes his turn to designate his successor by passing on the family blessing. Although Isaac will live another eighty years, this bestowal of the blessing is his last meaningful act recorded in the book of Genesis. But he fails the test of faithfulness in this task.

Abraham and Sarah had a single heir, Isaac. But for Isaac and Rebekah came twins to inherit the family legacy, Esau and Jacob. So the issue of which of the twins must carry forward the promises made to Abraham becomes a stumbling block requiring another intervention from God.

God speaks to Isaac's wife, Rebekah, at the birth of their sons, saying that the elder, Esau, would serve the younger, Jacob (25:23). This was contrary to the received wisdom of the day that the eldest must inherit the executive role in the family and its business dealings. Rather than cooperate with God's direction, Isaac actively opposes it.

 *Food for Thought*

For unstated reasons, Isaac disregards Rebekah's direction from the Lord. Sometimes in business we hear wisdom from those we don't consider to have the credentials to influence our decisions. How would you ensure that the wisdom of all the participants in your workplace might be acknowledged and considered?

_____

_____

_____

_____

_____

_____

_____

In Isaac's time, maintaining the family business meant that the fundamental structure of the family had to be intact. It was the father's job to secure this. Two related customs were prominent in Isaac's family, which might seem foreign to us today: the birthright (25:31) and the blessing (27:4).

The birthright conferred the right to inherit a larger share of the father's estate both in terms of goods and land. Although at times the birthright might be transferred, it was usually reserved for the firstborn son. The specific laws concerning it varied, but it seems to have been a steady feature of ancient Near Eastern culture. The birthright was associated with the father's blessing, which had to do with prosperity from God and dominion over the family.

Esau wrongly believes that he can surrender the birthright, yet still get the blessing (Heb. 12:16–17). Jacob recognizes that they are inseparable, and he also knows that with both in his possession, he can assume responsibility to carry on the heritage of the family, its faith, its work, and its social arrangements. He proves ambitious and self-confident.

Central to the unfolding plot of Genesis, the blessing entails not only receiving the covenantal promises that God had made to Abraham, but also mediating them to the next generation.

 Food for Thought

When it comes to succession, it seems that God disdains cookie-cutter attempts at "stability." What do you think God is looking for in choosing who gets a birthright and a blessing? Applying that, what do you think should matter in your workplace when it comes to promotions: seniority, talent, or something else? Why?

_____

_____

_____

_____

_____

_____

_____

Prayer

Pause for a few moments of silence to reflect on this lesson. Then offer a prayer, either spontaneous or by using the following:

Lord,

In Isaac's story we recognize our own blind spots when it comes to promoting people or seeking promotion ourselves. Please help us to see what you see, either in us as we seek promotion or in those we seek to promote. Help us find the right people or be the right people ourselves who will bring blessing to many others through our work.

Amen.

Lesson #3: Of Faith and Prejudice (27:1–46)

It seems to be a mark of human nature that we can play favorites when it comes to offspring or colleagues. For Isaac there is apparently some extra personal enjoyment that comes from his relationship with his son Esau, which makes him determined to ignore the direction of the Lord that came through Rebekah. Something about the manly outdoor lifestyle and Esau's provision of savory wild game cements the preference.

It is possible that Isaac knows Esau traded the birthright for a bowl of stew. If so, Isaac should be able to infer that Esau is not the person to lead the family enterprise. It is obvious to everyone else in the family that he has no interest in it. But against the evidence, Isaac wants Esau to have it.

Perhaps that's why Isaac makes the giving of the blessing a private affair. He has no idea Rebekah has overheard the plan, and so Jacob deceives him and gains the blessing and the right to lead. To Isaac's credit, his faith leads him to recognize that the divine blessing he mistakenly gives to Jacob was irrevocable. The writer of the New Testament letter to Hebrews explains with generosity, "By faith Isaac invoked future blessings on Jacob and Esau" (Heb. 11:20). And so we see that God chose Isaac to perpetuate this blessing and directed his will through him, despite Isaac's paternal favoritism.

For each of us, this story should resonate. In our closer relationships, the glow of personal enjoyment or the chill of displeasure can lead us into serious errors of judgment. This is especially so in matters of employing the right people for the right job. Our personal comforts, prejudices, and private interests can blind us to the wider importance of the work we are given to do.

Bias also operates at a systemic level. There are still many organizations that enable leaders to hire, fire, and promote people at their own whim, rather than following a long-term, coordinated, accountable process. By relying too much on personal networks, casual perceptions of performance, and individual mentoring to the exclusion of systematic training, organizations end up treating employees unfairly and squandering individual potential. They also perpetuate ethical, racial, class, gender, and other biases, to their own detriment.

Whether the abuses are individual or systemic, merely resolving to do better or to change organizational processes are not effective solutions. Instead, both individual hearts and organizational systems need to be transformed by God's grace.

Food for Thought

Can you identify weaknesses that can affect your judgment when it comes to conferring or receiving the blessing of promotion or employment? Perhaps the weakness is for accolades, dependence on others, conflict avoidance, people pleasing, prejudice or other factors that may be in opposition to God's purposes. Write them down by way of admission, and take a moment to ask God to help you reevaluate your perceptions. What could you do both personally and systematically to hold yourself more accountable in this area?

_____

_____

_____

_____

_____

_____

Prayer

Pause for a few moments of silence to reflect on this lesson. Then offer a prayer, either spontaneous or by using the following:

Lord,

We see that spiritual self-awareness is essential if we are to fulfill your purposes through our work. Grant us the grace to recognize how the attitudes with which we are so comfortable may be the enemy of your purposes and plans. Help us to want this renewal of our perceptions.

Amen.

Chapter 5

Jacob—Alienation and Return to Haran
(Genesis 28:1–29:35; 30:1–43)

"I am the LORD, the God of Abraham your father and the God of Isaac. The land on which you lie I will give to you and to your offspring. Your offspring shall be like the dust of the earth, and you shall spread abroad to the west and to the east and to the north and to the south, and in you and your offspring shall all the families of the earth be blessed. Behold, I am with you and will keep you wherever you go, and will bring you back to this land. For I will not leave you until I have done what I have promised you." (Gen. 28:13–15)

Lesson #1: Jacob and the Covenant (28:1–29:35)

When we see the names "Abraham, Isaac, and Jacob" grouped together in Scripture, it is because they each received the promises of God's covenant in their own generation and shared the same faith in him. Although separated generation to generation, they remained on the same page for the unfolding destiny of their family.

We have seen the characters of Abraham and Isaac, rescued from their weaknesses and brought to spiritual maturity through many handicaps and setbacks. But Abraham's grandson Jacob, born after Abraham's death and vested with leadership despite Isaac's opposition, brings a different circumstance and personality to the family story.

 *Food for Thought*

Imagine you are a young person in the camp of this family of God's covenant—what would you cling to in hearing the content of God's blessings to Abraham and Isaac? What would enable you want to lead the family enterprise forward in the same faith? What would give you pause?

_____

_____

_____

_____

_____

_____

_____

For most of the Genesis story, Jacob exhibits a cunning mind, and he uses it in grand deceptions, outwitting opponents and perceived enemies. Interestingly, he is also vulnerable to deception. In his ambition to gain his ends of birthright and blessing, a wife, a livelihood, and even reconciliation with his brother, he employs a complex playbook.

As we unfold Jacob's occupational life as a shepherd we will discover that his story has much to offer us as we develop a theology of work. Its significance is magnified because of the overarching trajectory of his life from alienation to reconciliation. We have seen that the work Abraham did was inseparable from the sense of purpose in his relationship with God. The same is true of Jacob, as it also should be for us.

 *Food for Thought*

As we approach the story of Jacob, it is useful to consider how we respond when we hit up against resistance to our goals. Argument? Confrontation? Politicking? Excommunication? Passive aggression? Simple retreat? Patience? An honest answer to the question may identify a perceived strength that we have come to use to manipulate others. Upon consideration, make notes on any insights gained into your own behavior, and suggest for yourself changes that you will pursue with the help of God's Spirit.

Prayer

Pause for a few moments of silence to reflect on this lesson. Then offer a prayer, either spontaneous or by using the following:

Lord,

We are so often blind to the effects of our behavior on others, especially so when we are passionate about pursuing our calling. It always seems so right. We acknowledge your command through the Apostle Paul to be transformed by the renewal of our minds. Help us to find truly ethical means to those goals we believe you have given us to accomplish.

Amen.

Lesson #2: The Fugitive Trickster (30:1–24)

It is one thing to agree with God's promise; it is another to trust him to bring it about. It seems we all have issues with waiting on the right time for an outcome, the time that God has ordained for fulfillment. Abraham and Sarah tried to shortcut the wait time for son Isaac by producing an heir themselves through Sarah's young slave, Hagar. The result was Ishmael and much domestic unhappiness.

Both Jacob and his mother Rebekah know of God's promise that Jacob will lead the family, but they resort to deception and theft to obtain it. This immediately endangers the family. For the safety of her son, Rebekah intercedes with her husband Isaac who then sends Jacob, with his blessing, back to the ancestral homeland of Haran to find a wife. In this way bloodshed between the brothers is averted. But the unethical means to God's intended end means that a long period of exile will ensue, entrenching a deep alienation within the family enterprise. It seems contrary to the plan and purpose of God that the family's future could be left in the hands of Esau, the brother least fit for the task.

 Food for Thought

What might Rebekah and Jacob have done differently? How difficult do you think that might have seemed to Jacob? From the previous lesson, how might you apply this ideal solution for Jacob to situations you may face in your workplace?

_____

_____

_____

_____

We discover in this reversal of fortune that God's promised blessings are gifts to be received, not grasped. We are not to hoard them; we are to use them for others. Though Jacob aspires to faith in the God of Abraham and Isaac, which he learned from his father, he depends on his own abilities to secure the privileges that accrue from that relationship.

While it may be commendable that Jacob values the birthright, he is quite foolish to try to secure it for himself by fraud. And so his fugitive departure from the family arises from pursuing a noble end through ignoble means.

En route to Haran, Jacob encounters God personally, which affirms his belief in God's covenant with his family. But his sojourn in Haran demonstrates his inability to trust God to act on his behalf. We see this in his conduct toward his uncle Laban, when he actually entraps himself in a long exile from Canaan. At this point in his life, it seems that Jacob allows his native wiliness to get the upper hand over his faith in God, rather than allowing his faith in God to bring change to his behavior, as his grandfather came to do.

He makes astute decisions with foxlike cunning that result in success, which we may be tempted to praise for their sheer effectiveness. But since his profit comes at the expense of exploiting and deceiving his uncle and cousins, we should know that something is awry. Although he has been wronged, can we be truly comfortable with his response, which is also a wrong? The Apostle Paul exhorts us to overcome evil with good (Rom. 12:21).

Unethical behavior often stems from fear. Jacob's relentless drive to acquire family and livelihood to replace what he left behind in Canaan reveals a deep-seated fear of exploitation (seen in the deception of his uncle Laban). This fear makes Jacob resist God's desire to bless him with the same undeserved graciousness offered to his father and grandfather.

To the extent we come to believe in and experience God's unconditional promises, we will be less inclined toward manipulating circumstances to benefit ourselves. The always present danger for us is our ability to fool ourselves, like Jacob, about the purity of our motives.

 Food for Thought

Often we feel a knee-jerk desire to right one wrong by perpetrating another. Identifying the underlying fear that triggers a vengeful response takes courage but brings great rewards in spiritual maturity. When we push through to facing the fear, we are able to bring it to the One who, when we confess it, proves faithful and just to forgive us and cleanse us from its inordinate effects (1 John 1:9). How do you respond ethically to a wrong?

_____

_____

_____

_____

_____

_____

_____

Prayer

Pause for a few moments of silence to reflect on this lesson. Then offer a prayer, either spontaneous or by using the following:

> *Lord,*
>
> *With our minds we recognize that from the beginning of Scripture you are revealed as gracious and forgiving of the sins of your people. Help us to treasure your unchanging character so that we might truly trust in you for dealing with our fears. Please help us discover the freedom to reflect your compassion in our dealings with others.*
>
> *Amen.*

Lesson #3: Hardball Entrepreneur (30:25–43)

Jacob's flight from his brother Esau brings him to the ancestral farm back in Haran, run by Laban, his mother's brother. Jacob works seven years for Laban in order to marry his cousin Rachel. So begins a string of his uncle's deceptions during twenty-one frustrating years.

Somehow, Laban disguises his other daughter, Leah, as Rachel so that after the wedding night Jacob awakes to find himself married to the wrong woman! A week later, Laban gives him an opportunity to also marry Rachel, but at the price of another seven years of work. When that time passes Jacob wants to return home, but Laban convinces him to stay on and work for him with the promise that he can name his own wages (30:28). It is clear from this offer that Jacob has helped Laban prosper without fair reward.

 *Food for Thought*

Fear has a way of blinding us to everything but the object of our fear. A means of identifying the hollowness of this object is to ask what are the "if only" items in our lives. For example, my life will be utterly fulfilled on this earth if only I could finish this book, if only I had a loving spouse, if only I could get that contract, if only I ace this project, and so on. Like Jacob, we are likely to react out of fear when we realize that something or someone threatens a goal on which we have pinned our hopes. To unmask this idolatry means freedom to reevaluate our relationship to God. What are some of your fears?

_____

_____

_____

_____

Once Jacob masters the art of selective breeding of animals to improve the herd, with that skill he devises a strategy to take revenge on Laban and his family, in order to enrich his own. His herd improves and multiplies, but Laban's herds weaken and diminish. Laban's sons complain with clarity, "Jacob has taken all that was our father's, and from what was our father's gained all this wealth" (31:1–2).

Although unable to understand how it happened, the grand deceiver, Laban, recognizes he was certainly outwitted by his nephew. Jacob puts a pious face on it by claiming the gain as a gift from God. He says, "If the God of my father, the God of Abraham and the Fear of Isaac, had not been on my side, surely now you would have sent me away empty-handed" (31:42). In a society that puts inordinate value on the maintenance of family honor, Laban, the leader, dares not admit publicly that he has been deceived. It's checkmate.

Thus Jacob makes another enemy in the same way he cheated Esau. What has he learned in twenty-one years? It seems the pattern is now fixed in Jacob's life. His father planned to take from him the blessing God had promised for him at birth, and Jacob reacted according to his mother's direction. Now, triggered by Laban's exploitation and the fear of losing more of what he counted for blessing, Jacob plays his own hardball. Then, adding insult to Laban's injury, he brings his religion into play as well. To credit God for his success as a schemer is probably Jacob's ultimate self-deception.

We don't see much integration of his faith with his work at this point, and it is worth noting that in the roll call of ancient faithfulness in that letter to the Hebrews, Jacob is mentioned only with respect to the behavior at the end of his life (Heb. 11:21).

 Food for Thought

Some people play hardball with people who have done them wrong. For others the signature act is a simple withdrawal. Some Christians doing these things are apt to put a pious face on it. We can justify aggression by saying, "It's tough love," or passive aggression with, "I can't dignify that with a response." How do you react to injustices in your workplace? Are there any changes you should make?

_____

_____

_____

_____

Prayer

Pause for a few moments of silence to reflect on this lesson. Then offer a prayer, either spontaneous or by using the following:

> *Lord,*
>
> *Please forgive us for justifying our hurtful words by pretending we're being pious. Grant that we might learn to agree with the letter of James: when all kinds of trials come against us, we will welcome them as friends, knowing that they come to prove our faith, which is more precious than gold. Help us to want the idols of our hearts exposed so that we leave behind our slavery to empty deception, to live and work in the blessing of your steadfast love.*
>
> *Amen.*

Chapter 6

Jacob—Leaving Laban, Embracing Esau

(Genesis 31:1–55; 32:1–32; 33:1–20)

So Jacob sent and called Rachel and Leah into the field where his flock was and said to them, "I see that your father does not regard me with favor as he did before. But the God of my father has been with me." (Gen. 31:4-5)

Lesson #1: Ending a Sour Business Relationship (31:1–55)

When Jacob separates his interests from Laban's, we find him attributing all the fury of his revenge to the justice of God. This includes the righteous indignation of his distress with Laban, justifying his strategy of fleeing in secret. So Jacob makes certain that his wives and servants adhere to his view that despite all his continuing deception, it is God who is now calling his father-in-law to full account, through him.

Laban will more simply justify all his behavior as the honorable duty of any good patriarch of a clan. He must retain ultimate power over Jacob's livelihood while Jacob remains in his territory. It seems in Laban's domain all rights accrue to him and his sons, while he makes a Cinderella of Jacob and Jacob's family.

 *Food for Thought*

Abusive relationships happen in business as well as in families, especially where family and business often coincide, in business partnerships and family companies. How did Jacob contribute to the abuse he suffered? Build on that and propose a better strategy for ending a business relationship.

_____

_____

_____

_____

_____

_____

It is worth noting how behavior is contagious, especially with those for whom we are responsible. Leah and Rachel mirror Jacob's tirade, railing against their father for robbing their husband while disinheriting them as daughters, along with their children. But Rachel takes her anger a bold step further. She seeks her own vengeance: without telling anyone, she steals her father's idols of gold. It proves to be a dangerous ploy.

The flight from Laban is true to Jacob's playbook. He escapes with his family and flocks while Laban is away shearing, and so he gains a three-day head start. Nonetheless, Laban and his sons pursue them, and it might have become ugly except that God, in his graciousness, appears to Laban in a dream to warn him against overreaction. Here at last is God intervening, true to himself, building toward a unique encounter with Jacob.

Laban overtakes the fugitive family and searches the tents of Jacob for the stolen idols. The stakes are raised as Jacob seeks to exonerate himself. He promises death to whoever is found to be the thief. Rachel hides them in a camel's saddle upon which she sits while declaring she is "in the way of women" (31:34). It's a successful ploy used against a religious charlatan with an ironic twist. His idols had for years deceived him with an inflated sense of his own honor and power, and in this moment he experiences neither honor nor power to stop what is happening. The estranged businessmen and in-laws part with a publicly executed covenant to stay out of each other's territory. Twenty-one years of unhealthy dealings between them now come to an end.

 Food for Thought

Jacob's behavior now echoes through Leah and Rachel—and to cast his hardball revenge on Laban as God's judgment on his rival has even a contemporary ring to it. But what is the significance of the way in which God acts in this story? How does it compare with Jacob's idea of God? How might that inform the way you deal with an unscrupulous boss or competitor?

_____

_____

_____

_____

_____

_____

_____

_____

Prayer

Pause for a few moments of silence to reflect on this lesson. Then offer a prayer, either spontaneous or by using the following:

Lord,

When we see our behavior repeated in those you give us to lead, we are often embarrassed to realize we've been excusing it in ourselves. And when we have excused it as a reflection of your character, it is even worse! Help us to escape our own schemes to gain certain ends, and to discover you as the One who says, "Ask and it will be given to you, seek and you will find, knock and the door will be opened." Thank you for your patience.

Amen.

Lesson #2: Encountering God (32:1–32)

When Jacob becomes free of his business attachment to his rich uncle, he is also free to return to Canaan and make peace with the man he originally cheated, his brother Esau. They have not seen each other in twenty-one years.

Jacob is now wealthy in his own right, perhaps attributing this to Isaac's blessing. And so it must also seem to him within his grasp to claim his birthright of leading the family of Abraham and Isaac. Despite the deception of two decades previous, Jacob sees an opportunity to legitimize his divinely appointed leadership by coming to an agreement with his estranged brother.

The content of the message he sends his brother to announce his coming suggests he expects negotiations to be tense. When the messengers report that Esau will soon arrive with four hundred armed men, this new scheme of Jacob's begins to look like a gamble going wrong.

Jacob splits his family and animals into two groups to help ensure some measure of survival. He prays for protection, and sends an enormous gift of animals on ahead of him, in staggered herds, in an effort to pacify Esau before the encounter.

 Food for Thought

By the gamble he took, it is clear that Jacob wants something far more than the wealth he gained by trickery in Haran. What do you think that is? Most of us look for more than material wealth out of our work—what is it you seek beyond your income? To what extent would you say that your faith in Christ has informed this motivation?

The night before he arrives at the meeting point, the trickster Jacob is visited by a shadowy figure who will turn the tables on him. God himself attacks him in the form of a strongman, against whom Jacob is forced to wrestle all night. It is not Esau or Laban he must contend with in regard to the future blessing of his family; it's the God of his father and grandfather—Isaac and Abraham. Here he discovers that God is not only the God of worship and piety, but also the God of work and family enterprises, and he will overpower even a slippery operator like Jacob.

So the Lord as Jacob's adversary presses his advantage to the point of permanently injuring Jacob's hip. Yet Jacob in this weakness says that he will not let go his grip on the stronger one until his attacker blesses him. He now knows with whom he is wrestling: the God of unbreakable promises.

We have arrived at the turning point of Jacob's life. Here after decades of self-deception, including religious self-deception, he meets God and receives the blessing he had tried to manipulate for himself. Jacob receives a new name, Israel ("God strives" and/or "he strives with God"), and he renames the location to fix it in the memory of his descendants that at this moment and in this place, he has seen the Almighty face to face (32:30).

 Food for Thought

It is sometimes said in mission agencies that Christian workers are not spiritually productive until they experience major disillusionment. To what extent does Jacob's story bear that out? What will you take away from his encounter with God that might inform the way you go about your work? What kind of "productivity" do you hope for now?

_____

_____

_____

_____

_____

_____

_____

_____

Prayer

Pause for a few moments of silence to reflect on this lesson. Then offer a prayer, either spontaneous or by using the following:

> *Lord,*
>
> *We so easily deceive ourselves in trite certainties operating in the business world. Help us to rely not on our brilliant techniques for productivity, but on knowing you better so as to pursue goals that you admire. Please help us know that in all we do we prove to be for you or against you. Let us pray with integrity your prayer: "Your kingdom come, your will be done, on earth as it is in heaven" (Matt. 6:10).*
>
> *Amen.*

Lesson #3: Reconciled Completely (33:1–20)

The detail in the encounter with Esau shows God intimately at work in the lives of his people, and Jacob in the beginnings of transformation. The fear of annihilation peaks with the appearance of Esau and four hundred men riding toward Jacob's camp. As if the gifts he sent on ahead must not have worked, Jacob leads his family forward in small groups from the servant girls and their children first, to his favorite wife and son placed last. He will intercede for their lives to be spared.

Such high-stakes appeasement proves unnecessary. Esau runs to Jacob and embraces him as one who has long forgiven the wrong. Although Esau graciously tries to refuse the extraordinary gift of so many animals, Jacob insists that he wants to bless Esau with it. When we hear him say, "Please accept my blessing that is brought to you, because God has dealt graciously with me, and because I have enough" (33:11), we can be confident that Jacob now counts knowing God more highly than his own achievements.

We can also know he really means it that to see his brother's face is like seeing the face of God, since with this moment of peaceful reunion the fear-filled years of imagined enmity fall to the ground.

 Food for Thought

An Irish saying goes: "The more you run from a ghost, the bigger it gets." Yet, as Jacob found, when you turn and face the thing you're afraid of, it can disappear. What fears do you or colleagues entertain in your own work life and how might you apply what you see in Jacob's story to deal with that? In what ways might you be able to see the face of God in the things you fear if you could let go of your fear of them?

_____

_____

_____

_____

_____

This reconciliation ends with an interesting footnote to Jacob's relationship with his brother Esau. There will be no rejoining of the separated family. Jacob, the wiser from his years with Laban, knows better than to merge the family enterprise with a brother who is not interested in the spiritual reality of God's covenantal purposes for the family. Esau may be militarily strong and prosperous, but Jacob journeys away from the apparent benefits of Esau's settlement at Seir and arrives outside the city of Shechem.

Here Jacob uses his wealth to purchase the land on which he seeks to encamp and, like Abraham before him, by implication he acknowledges the promise of owning the whole land in God's good time. He then celebrates God's deliverance of his family as the blessed line of Abraham and Isaac with a stone cairn—an altar of memorial—as another geographical witness to his descendants.

 Food for Thought

What do you make of Jacob's careful relocation away from his brother Esau? How might that caution apply in your own work environment? Have you experienced times when God seemed to lead you away from your family in order to pursue your work? Could there be times when it would be more in line with God's purposes to stay with your family, even if it prevents you from pursuing a promising work opportunity? Does anything in the story of Jacob and Esau help you determine which way God is leading you in any particular situation?

_____

_____

_____

_____

_____

So at the end of our study of Jacob's life we discover a truth that goes to the core of our faith: our relationships with God and people are linked, and both require humility and wisdom. Our reconciliation with God makes possible our reconciliation with others. Likewise, as we reconcile with others, we come to see and know God better.

The work of reconciliation applies to families, friends, churches, companies, and other forms of business, even people groups and nations. Springing from God's initial promise to Abraham, this is the blessing that Abraham's offspring, Jesus of Nazareth—Christ alone—has made available to the whole world. And we have opportunity to join his family enterprise as ambassadors for him.

 Food for Thought

So far we have seen three fallible human beings experience the reality of God and respond in different ways to establish the family line through which God's blessing will flow to the whole world. How has this informed you for your role in the enterprise of the family of God? Are there any changes you will be making in your approach to work in response to the stories of God acting in the lives of Abraham, Isaac, and Jacob?

_____

_____

_____

_____

_____

_____

Prayer

Pause for a few moments of silence to reflect on this lesson. Then offer a prayer, either spontaneous or by using the following:

Lord,

In the stories of Abraham, Isaac and Jacob, we've seen them act from distorted ideas of who you are. Yet rather than punish them, you persisted in blessing them and in Jacob's case even confronted him physically. Your actions show patient and steadfast love of those whom you call into your family. Thank you for choosing us to share in the blessings of Abraham's offspring, Christ our Savior. Grant that we will reflect your grace and engagement, in the work you give us to do and with the people you give to us as co-workers.

Amen.

Chapter 7

In the Footsteps of Abraham

Now the LORD said to Abram, "Go from your country and your kindred and your father's house to the land that I will show you. And I will make of you a great nation, and I will bless you and make your name great, so that you will be a blessing. I will bless those who bless you, and him who dishonors you I will curse, and in you all the families of the earth shall be blessed."

So Abram went, as the LORD had told him. (Gen. 12:1–4a)

Lesson #1: Bartholomaeus Ziegenbalg

The following case study is of a young German Lutheran, Bartholomaeus Ziegenbalg (1682–1719), who never finished his theological training. Yet by his simple obedience to God and the use of his giftedness as an entrepreneur, linguist, and teacher, he became a blessing to India in an extraordinary way. His story is finally reemerging from the sands of history.

By the age of eighteen, Bartholomaeus Ziegenbalg lost all his family to disease except for a younger sister. A chronic stomach illness marred his life in Germany, most likely the result of his poverty and high school years at a desk obsessively studying Greek, Hebrew, and Latin. Ironically, his illness meant he never completed a seminary degree. But he was an excellent teacher and found employment in experimental schools in Berlin.

Then, from left field at age twenty-two, he received a call through King Frederick IV of Denmark to go to the monarch's trading port in India (the Danish colony of Tranquebar) to work among the native Tamil people. At a time when most Europeans despised dark skinned peoples and had no theology of mission, Ziegenbalg received it as a call from God. By his entrepreneurial spirit he created institutions similar to a modern day NGO/aid agency (though more effective). In a short thirteen years, he laid a social foundation that would lift the Tamil people from ignorance and slavery, equipping them for an independent democracy in the twentieth century. But at the age of thirty-six, after a time of persecution by the Danish authorities and militant Hindus, he eventually died from his ill health.

Here are some of the blessings he brought in the name of Christ, the seed of Abraham:

- The state of Tamil Nadu today has a coeducational school system based on the twenty-three schools Ziegenbalg created in the early 1700s. Women did not receive education until he came to India.

- The printing and papermaking industry of India regards Ziegenbalg as its founder, since he established the first mechanized press and paper factory and employed Indians to run it.

- He developed a literary form of the Tamil vernacular language from the poetic classical Tamil script forbidden to all but the Brahmin caste. With that came a dictionary of 20,000 Tamil words and a grammar. His script is the literary form now used in Tamil newspapers and magazines.

- He was the first Indologist, and by his interest in understanding how Indians understood their religion and culture, he became a renowned expert throughout India for his practical knowledge of Indian life.

 *Food for Thought*

Have you ever thought what might have happened if Abraham had stayed in Haran and shied away from the adventure he was called to? Now consider: What adventure has been nudging you at the back of your consciousness, or perhaps it's in your face? How have you responded to it? Consider what might happen if you begin just step by step to move toward or simply do some research into that adventure.

_____

_____

_____

_____

_____

The list on the previous page describes only a few of the blessings for the Tamil people that came from Ziegenbalg's willingness to live and work in their land. But had he not gone, he may not have discovered his entrepreneurial giftedness in language, employment creation, and social reform. Although he might have succeeded as a teacher in Germany, it's more likely that he would have joined his family in an even earlier death from disease.

In July 2006, the federal government of India, along with the State of Tamil Nadu, promulgated a week of celebrations to recall his legacy to Tamil India. More than ten thousand Christians, Muslims, and Hindus made the pilgrimage to the site of the old Danish port where he is buried near the altar of the Jerusalem Church he dedicated a month before he died. A federal postage stamp was issued in his honor. More than four million Indians today can trace their spiritual heritage in Christ to the port town of Tharangambadi (or, in Danish, Tranquebar) where he lived and worked.

 Food for Thought

How many people can you recall who have made a significant impact? In what ways does this encourage you to reevaluate or pray for your call and personal mission in work? How can you make an impact on those around you?

_____

_____

_____

_____

_____

Prayer

Pause for a few moments of silence to reflect on this lesson. Then offer a prayer, either spontaneous or by using the following:

Lord,

Thank you for the people from the past whom we don't hear about, even though they followed you faithfully and by their faithfulness contributed something to the spiritual and social freedom and economic opportunity we enjoy. Grant that we might draw near to you and seek you so that we too may find your call on our lives and apply ourselves to the work you made us for. By faith, we know that only this kind of obedience will result in joyous celebration at the end of time.

Amen.

Lesson #2: Entertaining Angels

> [Abraham] said, "O Lord, if I have found favor in your sight, do not pass by your servant. Let a little water be brought, and wash your feet, and rest yourselves under the tree, while I bring a morsel of bread, that you may refresh yourselves, and after that you may pass on—since you have come to your servant." (Gen. 18:3–5)

The people of Tamil Nadu enjoy telling the story of how Ziegenbalg and his colleague Heinrich Plütschau arrived on the shores of Tharangambadi (Tranquebar).

Late one afternoon, the two young men came ashore after eight months at sea, and they discovered they were locked out of Fort Dansburg by the Danish East India Company governor. They didn't know he had orders from Copenhagen to destroy their work before they began it.

Like an Old Testament story, it was a Tamil servant of the governor who saw their plight and went to them on the beach to invite them into the slave quarter of the city. To the great surprise of the Tamil hosts, the two Europeans accepted the offer of hospitality as a divine gift and thanked their hosts for the generosity. It began a friendship that would beckon Ziegenbalg to live among and work for the Tamil slave population with all his entrepreneurial gifts for the remaining thirteen years of his life.

 Food for Thought

It is not a stretch to see Ziegenbalg and Plütschau as representatives of the blessing of Abraham through Christ, like angels entertained. Their glad welcome of the Tamil's hospitality was unique in the Danish colony, but it was the noble habit of the Tamils to greet people with this open offer of friendship. Can you see yourself as a representative of the blessing of Abraham too?

In what ways? Consider what would not have occurred if either party rejected the opportunity for hospitality.

_____

_____

_____

_____

_____

_____

Lesson #3: Freedom in Christ

> Abraham listened to Ephron, and Abraham weighed out for Ephron the silver that he had named in the hearing of the Hittites, four hundred shekels of silver, according to the weights current among the merchants. (Gen. 23:16)

There are times when Christians are required to challenge a particular cultural custom as Abraham did by refusing to enter into staged bargaining with Ephron. He offered transparency and generosity in its place.

For Ziegenbalg his challenge to Indian religion came when he had the respect of the Indians as Abraham had the respect of the Hittites. By creating schools for boys and for girls in the way that he learned in Berlin, he ignored the separation of caste and gender that had stultified Tamil life for millennia. Tamil life was mired in sex and labor slavery to the elite caste—sadly a contemporary issue in the globalized world today. And the East India Company exploited it to its own advantage.

Ziegenbalg not only produced the Bible in the Tamil script he developed, but he also printed classical Tamil literature about which most Tamils no idea until he made it available. He not only wanted them to be literate, but also to compare their own writings with the Scriptures. In this way, they could discover the God who wanted to bless them with the personal relationship that their literature showed that they longed for but hadn't experienced. In his lifetime, 250 Tamils joined his church. It was enough to help generations of Tamils provide their own improvements in health, government, economics, arts—literally everything that made up their culture. Eventually, they became a free, self-governing people.

 Food for Thought

When our work is framed in the context of God's eternal purposing, it becomes a catalyst for redeeming human life in our particular time and place. It is no longer a lifeless duty but a vital service to the human race, even if it creates enemies. What surprises you in Ziegenbalg's story, and how does it relate to the Genesis family enterprise thus far?

_____

_____

_____

_____

_____

_____

_____

Prayer

Pause for a few moments of silence to reflect on this final chapter. Then offer a prayer, either spontaneous, or by using the following:

Lord,

We long to be found faithful in the family business of our Lord Jesus Christ. And we can see from the family of Abraham, and from Ziegenbalg and his Tamil friends, that our lives are meant to be integrated with your Spirit informing everything we do, including our work and our relating to others. Please assist us to be fearless in vital service to our neighbors, colleagues, and co-workers, as well as our family. Make us the blessing you intended so that celebration is the end point of everything we do until your kingdom is fully come.

Amen.

Summary: Building the Family Business to Bless the Earth

By faith Abraham obeyed when he was called to go out to a place that he was to receive as an inheritance. And he went out, not knowing where he was going. By faith he went to live in tents with Isaac and Jacob, heirs with him of the same promise. (Heb. 11:8-9)

In studying Genesis 12–33 we have discovered the story of the first three generations of the family—Abraham, Isaac, and Jacob—through whom God chose to bring blessing to the whole world.

Having no particular power, position, wealth, fame, ability, or moral superiority of their own, they became leaders of a semi-nomadic enterprise. Each member of the family began to receive God's blessing by accepting God's call to trust him to provide for them and fulfill the great vision he had for them.

After some questionable moments while seeking economic opportunities in Egypt, their obedience led them to endure the hardships of making a living as newcomers in an already settled land, Canaan. They persevered because God promised and reconfirmed to each generation that their descendants would eventually own the entire length and breadth of Canaan.

 *Food for Thought*

To what extent is Abraham's story an immigrant story? If you think it is, what might it offer by way of wisdom applicable to immigrant people seeking to earn a living in a new land? And what might it offer as wisdom applicable to business people who are citizens of the land, especially in relation to newcomers?

_____

_____

_____

_____

_____

Have you noticed that each time God appears in the narratives of these three generations, his actions demonstrate steadfast commitment to their well-being, even when we might expect that they deserve serious rebuke and punishment? We should be encouraged. God proved faithful and patient in every way, despite their failures of faith, which were shown at times to be fitful, timid, foolish, and even misguided.

They proved to be as dysfunctional as any family, yet they developed a faithful reliance upon God's promises. Functioning in a broken world, surrounded by hostile people and powers, by faith they "invoked future blessings" and lived according to God's promises, says the writer of Hebrews 11:20. "Therefore God is not ashamed to be called their God, for he has prepared for them a city" (Heb. 11:16)—the same city toward which we also work as followers of "Jesus Christ, the son of David, the son of Abraham" (Matt. 1:1).

 *Food for Thought*

Recall the most vivid insight you have gained from this study and consider how you will apply it to your own life, especially in your workplace.

_____

_____

_____

_____

_____

_____

_____

Prayer

Pause for a few moments of silence to reflect on this summary. Then offer a prayer, either spontaneous or by using the following:

Lord,

When we consider our spiritual forebears in Genesis— Abraham and Sarah, Isaac and Rebekah, and Jacob, Leah, and Rachel—we can't help noticing how gentle and kind you were with them in their frailty as people, and how they responded to this with renewed faithfulness each time they wandered from your path. Please assist us to recognize that it's your kindness that led us to repentance, and make us able to offer this same patient kindness to those we work with by your Spirit.

Amen.

Wisdom for Using This Study in the Workplace

Community within the workplace is a good thing and a Christian community within the workplace is even better. Sensitivity is needed, however, when we get together in the workplace (even a Christian workplace) to enjoy fellowship time together, learn what the Bible has to say about our work, and encourage one another in Jesus' name. When you meet at your place of employment, here are some guidelines to keep in mind:

- Be sensitive to your surroundings. Know your company policy about having such a group on company property. Make sure not to give the impression that this is a secret or exclusive group.

- Be sensitive to time constraints. Don't go over your allotted time. Don't be late to work! Make sure you are a good witness to the others (especially non-Christians) in your workplace by being fully committed to your work during working hours and doing all your work with excellence.

- Be sensitive to the shy or silent members of your group. Encourage everyone in the group and give them a chance to talk.

- Be sensitive to the others by being prepared. Read the Bible study material and Scripture passages and think about your answers to the questions ahead of time.

These Bible studies are based on the Theology of Work biblical commentary. Besides reading the commentary, please visit the Theology of Work website (www.theologyofwork.org) for videos, interviews, and other material on the Bible and your work.

Leader's Guide

Living Word. It is always exciting to start a new group and study. The possibilities of growth and relationship are limitless when we engage with one another and with God's word. Always remember that God's word is "alive and active, sharper than any double-edged sword" (Heb. 4:12) and when you study his word, it should change you.

A Way Has Been Made. Please know you and each person joining your study have been prayed for by people you will probably never meet but who share your faith. And remember that "the LORD himself goes before you and will be with you; he will never leave you nor forsake you. Do not be afraid; do not be discouraged" (Deut. 31:8). As a leader, you need to know that truth. Remind yourself of it throughout this study.

Pray. It is always a good idea to pray for your study and those involved weeks before you even begin. It is recommended to pray for yourself as leader, your group members, and the time you are about to spend together. It's no small thing you are about to start and the more you prepare in the Spirit, the better. Apart from Jesus, we can do nothing (John 14:5). Remain in him and "you will bear much fruit" (John 15:5). It's also a good idea to have trusted friends pray and intercede for you and your group as you work through the study.

Spiritual Battle. Like it or not, the Bible teaches that we are in the middle of a spiritual battle. The enemy would like nothing more than for this study to be ineffective. It would be part of his scheme to have group members not show up or engage in any discussion. His victory would be that your group just passes time together going through the motions of just another Bible study. You, as a leader, are a threat to the enemy as it is your desire to lead people down the path of righteousness (as taught in Proverbs). Read Ephesians 6:10–20 and put your armor on.

Scripture. Prepare before your study by reading the selected Scripture verses ahead of time.

Chapters. Each chapter contains approximately three lessons. As you work through the lessons, keep in mind the particular chapter theme in connection with the lessons. These lessons are designed so that you can go through them in thirty minutes each.

Lessons. Each lesson has teaching points with their own discussion questions. This format should keep the participants engaged with the text and one another.

Food for Thought. The questions at the end of the teaching points are there to create discussion and deepen the connection between each person and the content being addressed. You know the people in your group and should feel free to come up with your own questions or adapt the ones provided to best meet the needs of your group. Again, this would require some preparation beforehand.

Opening and Closing Prayers. Sometimes prayer prompts are given before and usually after each lesson. These are just suggestions. You know your group and the needs present, so please feel free to pray accordingly.

Bible Commentary. The Theology of Work series contains a variety of books to help you apply the Scriptures and Christian faith to your work. This Bible study is based on the *Theology of Work Bible Commentary*, examining what the Bible says about work. This commentary is intended to assist those with theological training or interest to conduct in-depth research into passages or books of Scripture.

Video Clips. The Theology of Work website (www.theologyofwork .org) provides good video footage of people from the marketplace highlighting the teaching from all the books of the Bible. It would be great to incorporate some of these videos into your teaching time.

Enjoy Your Study! Remember that God's word does not return void—ever. It produces fruit and succeeds in whatever way God has intended it to succeed.

> "So shall my word be that goes out from my mouth;
>> it shall not return to me empty,
> but it shall accomplish that which I purpose,
>> and shall succeed in the thing for which I sent it." (Isa. 55:11)

"This commentary was written exactly for those of us who aim to integrate our faith and work on a daily basis and is an excellent reminder that God hasn't called the world to go to the church, but has called the Church to go to the world."

BONNIE WURZBACHER

FORMER SENIOR VICE PRESIDENT, THE COCA-COLA COMPANY